# ALL ABOUT
# Wolverines

T0151496

WRITTEN BY
## Jordan Hoffman

Wolverine

2

Have you ever seen a wolverine?

Wolverines are mammals. They are related to weasels, but wolverines are much larger. Wolverines can grow to between 80 and 110 centimetres long and stand between 66 and 86 centimetres tall.

**Weasel**

Wolverines have dark brown fur with two lighter stripes along their bodies. They also usually have white or orange patches on their chests. Their fur is long and thick.

Wolverines have a wide head with small black eyes, short, round ears, and a dark snout.

Wolverines have very strong bodies with lots of muscle. Wolverines weigh about 10 to 15 kilograms. That is about the same weight as a medium-sized dog.

There are differences between male and female wolverines.

Male wolverines are longer, taller, and heavier than females.

Male wolverines also travel much farther than females.

Wolverines can be found in forests, mountainous areas, and on the tundra. They are usually found away from communities and people.

Wolverines can travel long distances each day in search of food. They sometimes even climb high mountains to find areas with food.

In Nunavut, you can find wolverines near communities such as Kugluktuk and Taloyoak.

Wolverines are harvested for their fur. Their fur is often used on the hoods of parkas. This is because it does not collect ice and is very warm.

Wolverines are **omnivores** that eat many different types of animals and plants. Wolverines mostly eat meat, but in the summer they sometimes eat plants and berries.

Wolverines feed on **prey** such as siksiks, Arctic hares, geese, and lemmings. Wolverines can also hunt animals much larger than them, such as caribou.

Wolverines often find food left behind by other predators, such as Arctic foxes, wolves, and grizzly bears. This behaviour is called **scavenging**.

Wolverines can survive for long periods without food. They sometimes hide food in the snow. Wolverines will go back to areas where they stored food for a meal.

Female wolverines build dens in the snow. This is where they give birth to their young. They often build their dens in areas with boulders. This is to protect their young from **predators** and harsh weather.

A female wolverine going into her den

19

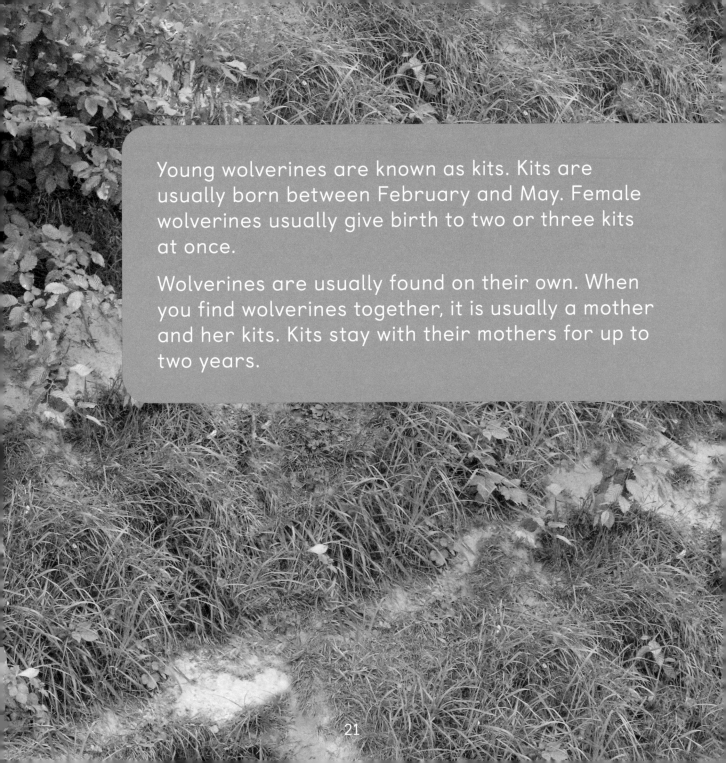

Young wolverines are known as kits. Kits are usually born between February and May. Female wolverines usually give birth to two or three kits at once.

Wolverines are usually found on their own. When you find wolverines together, it is usually a mother and her kits. Kits stay with their mothers for up to two years.

Wolverines leave a strong-smelling scent on their food and in areas where they live. This scent keeps other wolverines and animals away.

Wolverines are sometimes called skunk bears because they look like small bears and leave a strong-smelling scent like skunks.

Wolverines are one of Nunavut's incredible animals. They are skilled hunters and can travel long distances. Their fur can be used to make warm, beautiful parkas. What do you like most about wolverines?

## Glossary

**omnivore**
an animal that eats both plants and other animals.

**predators**
animals that hunt other animals.

**prey**
an animal that is hunted by another animal.

**scavenging**
feeding on dead animals.

Nunavummi